BANTAMS
FOR EGGS

By C. G. MAY

SECOND EDITION

British Library Cataloguing-in-Publication Data
A catalogue record for this book is available from the
British Library

Poultry Farming

Poultry farming is the raising of domesticated birds such as chickens, turkeys, ducks, and geese, for the purpose of farming meat or eggs for food. Poultry are farmed in great numbers with chickens being the most numerous. More than 50 billion chickens are raised annually as a source of food, for both their meat and their eggs. Chickens raised for eggs are usually called 'layers' while chickens raised for meat are often called 'broilers'. In total, the UK alone consumes over 29 million eggs per day

According to the Worldwatch Institute, 74% of the world's poultry meat, and 68% of eggs are produced in ways that are described as 'intensive'. One alternative to intensive poultry farming is free-range farming using much lower stocking densities. This type of farming allows chickens to roam freely for a period of the day, although they are usually confined in sheds at night to protect them from predators or kept indoors if the weather is particularly bad. In the UK, the Department for Environment, Food and Rural Affairs (Defra) states that a free-range chicken must have day-time access to open-air runs during at least half of its life. Thankfully, free-range farming of egg-laying hens is increasing its share of the market. Defra figures indicate that 45% of eggs produced in the UK throughout 2010 were free-range, 5% were produced in barn systems and 50% from cages. This compares with 41% being free-range in 2009.

Despite this increase, unfortunately most birds are still reared and bred in 'intensive' conditions. Commercial hens usually begin laying eggs at 16–20 weeks of age, although production gradually declines soon after from approximately 25 weeks of age. This means that in many countries, by approximately 72 weeks of age, flocks are considered economically unviable and are slaughtered after approximately 12 months of egg production. This is despite the fact that chickens will naturally live for 6 or more years. In some countries, hens are 'force molted' to re-invigorate egg-laying. This practice is performed on a large commercial scale by artificially provoking a complete flock of hens to molt simultaneously. This is usually achieved by withdrawal of feed for 7-14 days which has the effect of allowing the hen's reproductive tracts to regress and rejuvenate. After a molt, the hen's production rate usually peaks slightly below the previous peak rate and egg quality is improved. In the UK, the Department for Environment, Food and Rural Affairs states 'In no circumstances may birds be induced to moult by withholding feed and water.' Sadly, this is not the case in all countries however.

Other practices in chicken farming include 'beak trimming', this involves cutting the hen's beak when they are born, to reduce the damaging effects of aggression, feather pecking and cannibalism. Scientific studies have shown that such practices are likely to cause both acute and chronic pain though, as the beak is a complex, functional organ with an extensive nervous supply. Behavioural evidence of pain after beak trimming in layer hen chicks has been based on the observed reduction in pecking behaviour, reduced activity and social behaviour, and increased sleep duration. Modern egg laying breeds also frequently suffer from osteoporosis which results in the chicken's skeletal system being weakened. During egg production, large amounts of calcium are transferred from bones to create egg-shell. Although dietary calcium levels are adequate, absorption of dietary calcium is not always sufficient, given the intensity of production, to fully replenish bone calcium. This can lead to increases in bone breakages, particularly when the hens are being removed from cages at the end of laying.

The majority of hens in many countries are reared in battery cages, although the European Union Council Directive 1999/74/EC has banned the conventional battery cage in EU states from January 2012. These are small cages, usually made of metal in modern systems, housing 3 to 8 hens. The walls are made of either solid metal or mesh, and the floor is sloped wire mesh to allow the faeces to drop through and eggs to roll onto an egg-collecting conveyor belt. Water is usually provided by overhead nipple systems, and food in a trough along the front of the cage replenished at regular intervals by a mechanical chain. The cages are arranged in long rows as multiple tiers, often with cages back-to-back (hence the term 'battery cage'). Within a single shed, there may be several floors contain battery cages meaning that a single shed may contain many tens of thousands of hens. In response to tightened legislation, development of prototype commercial furnished cage systems began in the 1980s. Furnished cages, sometimes called 'enriched' or 'modified' cages, are cages for egg laying hens which have been designed to overcome some of the welfare concerns of battery cages whilst retaining their economic and husbandry advantages, and also provide some of the welfare advantages of non-cage systems.

Many design features of furnished cages have been incorporated because research in animal welfare science has shown them to be of benefit to the hens. In the UK, the Defra 'Code for the Welfare of Laying Hens' states furnished cages should provide at least 750 cm² of cage area per hen, 600 cm² of which should be usable; the height of the cage other than that above the usable area should be at least 20 cm at every point and no cage should have a total area that is less than 2000 cm². In addition, furnished cages should provide a nest, litter such that pecking and scratching are possible, appropriate perches allowing at least 15 cm per hen, a claw-shortening device, and a feed trough which may be used without restriction providing 12 cm per hen. The practice of chicken farming continues to be a much debated area, and it is hoped that in this increasingly globalised and environmentally aware age, the inhumane side of chicken farming will cease. There are many thousands of chicken farms (and individual keepers) that treat their chickens with the requisite care and attention, and thankfully, these numbers are increasing.

CONTENTS

ILLUSTRATIONS

INTRODUCTION

THIS book was originally produced in wartime. For this reason it will depart from many of the accepted methods of feeding and general management accorded to miniature breeds of poultry.

In normal times the breeder of bantams is mainly concerned with keeping down the size of his charges; give him a Wyandotte that " bumps " the scale down at an ounce or so over the standard weight, or a Rhode Island Red that is more than one third the size of its counterpart in large fowls, and you would never hear the end of it. Hear also what he would say if he were offered a Sussex with lots of black feathers in its back !

Production of mongrels will not be tolerated, but the chapter on feeding will pay little regard to standard weights. Neither shall I insist that every wartime bantam should be able to score 80 points out of a maximum 100 for its breed characteristics. In short, I intend to deal with the bantam as a utility fowl rather than as a work of art for the show pen.

Strong Utility Claim

Yes, bantams have every claim to be regarded from utility angles and, small as they are, they can play, and must play, an important part in the production of food—both in the shape of eggs and plump little cockerels for the table.

Cuts in the domestic poultry ration have done more than anything to turn the spotlight on to bantams and it is in their favour that officially a bantam is a domestic fowl and is, therefore, entitled to receive the ration of a full-size hen. I must add, rather hastily, that shell egg registrations have to be surrendered to enable the owners of bantams to draw rations for their birds in just the same manner as is necessary for other classes of poultry.

Greatest advantage is that at least six bantams could be kept on the amount of food which would be consumed by three ordinary hens ; that is, of course, provided you go the right way about it. This little book will do its best to help you.

3

Utility bantams are not new. My first contact with them was back in the very early " twenties " when the National Utility Poultry Society ran its show in the Horticultural Hall, Vincent Square, Westminster. Secretary Mrs. Rawson and her Committee surprised showmen by putting on a class or two for utility bantams. The classes filled and, very soon, the idea was copied by other progressive societies. At one of the Westminster shows a class for bantam eggs was provided and visitors just would not believe that the entries were from bantams until they saw similar eggs produced by the birds on show.

Although the British Bantam Association has not gone out of its way to encourage the utility bantam, it is worth observing that " utility qualities " are frequently mentioned in the Association's pre-war Year Books, while its Secretary, now closely associated with D.P.K.C. work, never tires of boosting his favourites.

All-round Economy

Economy with foodstuffs has already been mentioned. Bantams are also economical in housing and the appliances they need. An ordinary house designed to accommodate four or five large fowl could easily be made to hold nearly twice as many bantams.

In pre-war days a pen of bantams came to be regarded as the stepping stone to something bigger. A show expert would start his young son off with a few miniature fowl, knowing that their charm, their docility and their capability to produce eggs would make the youngster keen. I have not the slightest doubt that those who turn to bantams now in an effort to help out with table produce will not want to discard them when a world of real peace and plenty returns.

C. G. M.

CHAPTER I

UTILITY VALUE OF BANTAMS

WHAT is a bantam? My dictionary says that it is " a small variety of the common domestic fowl." If I were asked to give a clearer definition I would, without hesitation, say that a bantam is the counterpart, in miniature, of a pure-bred fowl.

There is, I hope, a vast difference between a common

It is freely admitted that the Old English Game has played a part in the " manufacture " of Rhode Island Red bantams. This photograph is of a Black-red O.E.G. bantam cockerel.

and a pure-bred fowl, and while we all can see much to admire in our sex-linked and commercial crosses in big breeds, there are very few who would tolerate similar developments in bantams.

I repeat that which has been recorded in the introduction : This is not a book written to extol the virtues of show bantams ; it is a wartime publication intended to rivet attention on the utility properties of these miniature fowls. At the same time, it will respect many of those things that the pre-war fancier respects ; among them will be the question of keeping the breeds pure.

How were bantams first introduced ? Some of them came to us ready-made and are obviously the products of judicious crossing of large breeds and out-of-season breeding. Others, and they include varieties made in this country, have been bred down from the large fowl without introducing the blood of any outside breed.

A   5

To make this point clear I give a brief resume of what I know two breeders of Rhode Island Red bantams have done to establish their own strains.

One was prepared to take his time and he decided to breed down from the big fowl.   He selected a few of his smallest Rhode Island Red hens of a late-season hatch and mated them to a small, but vigorous, cockerel.   The hens were not weaklings, they were strong and virile, but their growth had obviously been hindered because part of it, due to late-hatching, was carried out in winter.

The smaller off-spring were mated back to their father while the larger were put with a pure Rhode bantam of another strain. This gave their breeder two distinct lines of what he called " first generation bantams " to work upon and he then com-menced mixing.

To aid a speedy re-duction of size he set himself the task of producing two gene-rations in a season,

The " showman " would probably say that this little Rhode Island Red male is too heavy in headgear. The utility breeder overlooks this and would welcome him at the head of the pen.

which meant, of course, breeding from pullets that had been helped along the road to early production.   It took him five years to get his strain fully established and, apart from the outside purchase of a ready-made bantam in the early stages, no other blood or breed figured in its making.

Breeder No. 2 was in a hurry.   He chose, as a short cut to success, his smallest Rhode pullets from the big pens and mated them to a vigorous Old English Game bantam cock.   Offspring from this mating were put to one of those small " grandfather " Rhode cockerels which are common in many utility strains. Pullets from this pen were mated back to cockerels from the first lot, *i.e.*—Rhode cross O.E.G. Two seasons of out-crossing were sufficient to provide him with his own strain of Rhode Bantams.

A breeder of Light Sussex, with whom I am acquainted, took six years to breed his down from the big Sussex. His patience has, however, been more than rewarded because he is now at the head of breeders of this variety.

A miniature of the large Sussex fowl. This, with the Rhode Island Red, the Ancona and the Minorca is regarded as one of the best of the utility breeds of bantams.

Those who aspire to produce their own strains of bantams should bear one fact more than any other in mind—while reduction in size is of first importance, it cannot be attained by breeding from weaklings or birds that have been stunted in growth by unnatural means. Grain feeding as opposed to mash will also play a not unimportant part.

What effect will this breeding-down have upon egg size ? Precisely the opposite from that which might be expected. A big Sussex weighing up to eight lbs. will produce $2\frac{1}{4}$-$2\frac{1}{2}$ oz. eggs ; a Sussex bantam, which would have difficulty in turning the scale at two lbs. will give eggs of $1\frac{1}{2}$ or even $1\frac{3}{4}$ oz. with precisely the same regularity.

It is, of course, said that the egg of a bantam is twice as rich as that of a big fowl, but this is praise which should be taken with a grain of salt. What is an established fact is that many housewives prefer bantam to hen eggs for cake making.

A question often asked, and it is one that is easy to answer, is whether egg production among the miniatures is seasonal. With some birds the reply is in the affirmative, but with the recognised laying breeds the answer is that production is fairly evenly spread over the entire year. There will, of course, always be the Spring and early Summer flush.

One astonishing feature with bantams is that some of the breeds which are not regarded as egg producers in big fowl are just the opposite in miniatures. I give one outstanding instance in my own experience of them.

"My respect for the Frizzle, a purely exhibition breed, rose sky-high." Here is a typical little Blue Frizzle hen, showing the quaint feather curl seen only in this breed.

In 1939 I was asked to take the British Livestock Exhibit to the World's Poultry Congress in Cleveland, Ohio, U.S.A. Among the 200-odd birds were a pair of Buff Frizzle bantams. These little pullets were in lay on their arrival at the assembly centre in London ; they were still hard at it for the ten days' ocean journey. A two-day train journey from Montreal down to Cleveland had no effect at all upon them and they continued to lay throughout the ten days of the exhibition.

They certainly were an exceptional pair, but had I not seen this with my own eyes I should have regarded the story as somewhat far-fetched. My respect for the Frizzle, a purely exhibition breed, rose sky high.

With regard to winter production, I have in front of me the trapped records of four Light Sussex bantam pullets for October, 1942. Here they are : Blue ring—21 eggs ; Green—23 ; Yellow—18 ; Red—15. The little green-ring pullet laid 13 eggs without a break and a fact worth recording is that her output of 23 in 31 days represented almost exactly her own body weight. Her eggs averaged

A TRIO OF PERKY BANTAM COCKERELS

BARRED ROCK   BLACK MINORCA   ANCONA

Perfect miniatures of large fowl these three varieties recommend themselves to the wartime bantam breeder.

a mere fraction below $1\frac{1}{2}$ oz. each and her weight was just under 2 lb.

This, again, was an exceptional performance. What was also exceptional was that it was done on a wartime diet.

It is, of course, only fair to add that sudden spells of cold weather will possibly get a bantam under quicker than a large fowl. It is in this direction that management and

AND HERE ARE THREE PULLETS

COLUMBIAN   PARTRIDGE   WHITE

All members of the Wyandotte family, they can be successfully bred in quarters that would prove far too restricted for large fowl.

comfortable housing will play a major part and, even at the risk of repetition in the chapter on housing, here are a few hints to ensure comfort :

Provide a good depth of soft, dry scratching litter in both house and run. Remember the vagaries of the British climate and board up the lower part of the run (glass is even better because it admits light) to keep out the driving rain. If no run is provided use glass lights at the front and rear of the six-by-four or whatever type of house is to be used.

Keep the birds under cover during bad weather. A soaking with rain is hardly conducive to egg production, neither is a prolonged run out on frozen grass. When liberty is restricted provide anything as a scratch feed in the litter to keep the birds busy and to prevent overfatness.

Portable Lawns

An excellent idea that I have often come across is for the bantam keeper to fit freshly-cut grass turves into a few ordinary seed boxes. One box is put into the house to-day and is replaced by a fresh one tomorrow. By the time the whole series of boxes have been used the first has grown a fresh crop of grass and is ready for use again.

This opening chapter will, I hope, have given the reader an insight into bantam possibilities. Now to the more serious work of their management.

CHAPTER II

HOUSING AND GENERAL MANAGEMENT

F there is one thing above all else that bantams must be given, it is comfortable quarters. The last impression I desire to create is that, because they are small they are weak ; well bred, well fed and well housed they are strong and virile, but their very nature leaves them open to troubles which might not affect their counterpart in large fowl.

I hope to illustrate this chapter with types of houses eminently suitable for bantams and they will, without doubt, include the much boosted and seldom found wanting

Seen in the Ministry of Information Poultry Film this house was once a summer house. It has been converted to accommodate four large fowl, but it could easily hold eight bantams. Floor space gives roughly 24 square feet and the roosting compartment, on the left, is fitted with two perches running from front to rear. The outside fitments are—top : nest boxes ; below : closed-in hopper, to accommodate food trough and grit box. Window is re-inforced netted glass. Squared trellis work—made from laths —takes the place of ordinary wire netting.

six-by-four lean-to. There will also be a two-storey house on a raised platform and portable outside runs.

I have seen bantams kept successfully in houses not much larger than rabbit hutches, but I do sincerely hope that no reader of this book will want to keep them in batteries !

It goes without saying that if they can be given a grass run they will appreciate it to the full, but there is no need to become disheartened if the nearest grass patch is a mile distant—bantams will do excellently on an earth or littered floor.

Space is not nearly so necessary with them as with big fowl. Where one is normally disposed to suggest that not less than four square feet of floor space is required for an ordinary pullet, a bantam will thrive on two square feet. But remember, always, that exercise with them is as important as it is with the larger varieties and the space given them for this purpose should not be restricted just because I have written two square feet per bird. The run of a garden will, indeed, prove most economical from the feeding point of view.

Rabbits Out—Bantams In

One very excellent plan I have seen adopted is turning over to a trio of bantams a disused Morant rabbit hutch. The only alterations needed were a perch in the sleeping compartment, a couple of outside nest boxes also at the roosting end and the removal of the wire-netted floor in the run. Moved to fresh spots every other day the grass on which these bantams were run was distinctly improved. The system is, in fact, the fold system of poultry-keeping in miniature.

A six-by-four gives a floor space of 24 square feet. At the rate of two square feet per bird it should, therefore, accommodate 12 bantams. But I suggest that a happy medium be struck and that only nine should be turned in. If part of the floor space is occupied by nests, troughs or drinkers, be content with six birds. These reckonings are made with full regard to any outside run that the bantams may have. No matter how large the garden or the uncovered run, they *must* be given a minimum of two square feet per bird of housing space.

Like most other things ready-made houses are in limited supply and many prospective bantam keepers will be tempted to make their own. The fact that large buildings are not needed is in their favour, as this means that short lengths of timber can be used. A couple of fair-sized packing cases would break the back of the job and, scarce as these may be, they can be found !

Asbestos cement is not in unlimited supply and if some is obtained it can be used for ends and roof.

Most fortunate person is the one who has a small out-

Double-storied, with the run portion underneath, this is another type of six-by-four. It is the popular " Seaford Utility " house and gives excellent accommodation for six to eight bantams or for a breeding pen of one male and four females.

house that can be converted, and on page 11 I have taken the liberty of " lifting " from the Ministry of Information film a shot of an excellent little summer-house, complete with lattice work, that would make ideal accommodation for half-a-dozen bantams.

Simple rules to follow in the make-up of a house are these :

Where floors are provided it is always best to raise the house off ground level on brick or small concrete piles. Main idea behind this is not, as many think, to keep away vermin but to maintain a dry floor.

Do not skimp the slope to the roof. A house of four feet six inches frontal height, and with a depth of four feet, should gave a six-inch slope to the rear. This means, of course, that the height at the back should be four feet.

A minimum of six inches of perch space should be allowed for each bird and, rather than erect two short perches, put in one long one. With two perches it is usually found that the birds will crowd on one and leave the other unoccupied.

Give six birds a three-compartment nest box, each compartment being not less than nine inches square. If all the bantams crowd into one compartment remove the divisions and make the box a communal one. This is a far better plan than running the risk of having eggs broken in the nest.

South-East, but Watch Rain

A south-easterly position is reckoned to be the best, only drawback with it is that rain often blows from that quarter ! Which fact is a good enough excuse to repeat the advice in a previous chapter to board up the lower part of the run to help keep out this driving rain.

To revert to grass or a garden run. Bantams are not destructive to the extent that larger fowl are. Turn them loose in a patch of young cabbage plants and they will certainly play a merry game, but in and out of a flower garden they do very little harm. It is not necessary that they should have the run of the garden all the time—an hour or so in the morning and again in the afternoon will find them scratching here, there and everywhere for natural foods. I have watched them strip green-fly off rose bushes without breaking down a single shoot.

Certainly they will find a cool, damp spot for a dust bath and, if permitted to do so, will return to the spot each day. The disturbance of the soil they create is infinitesimal compared with that of large fowl.

On a piece of grass they are very happy. A little portable run which takes them up and down a lawn is a worthwhile addition to the owner's equipment. They scratch the grass without damaging it, they manure the ground and woe betide earth worms that come to the surface ! Use a small patch of grass at a time and move the run to a fresh spot every day or every other day. The same run can, of course, be put on any uncultivated part of the kitchen

An outdoor aviary accommodates these Old English Game bantams and the " Budgies " are not dispossessed ! From this and the other photographs it will be seen that bantams can be successfully kept in a variety of houses—they are, in fact, " at home," anywhere.

garden or on those parts that are being rested temporarily. Here, again, there is the advantage of manure.

Where no garden run is available try to give the wee ones a small run on their six-by-four or whatever type of house is adopted. Let it be covered during the bad months or during long spells of rain, but open it up to sun when conditions are favourable.

Under those conditions where the bantams must be restricted entirely to their house, give them a good depth of dry scratching litter in which they will not hesitate to exercise. A clod of fresh clean earth or a turf of grass dropped in the house at regular intervals will keep them occupied for hours. Do not misunderstand me and put in roots of rough old grass that will easily cause crop troubles —what is wanted is a nice fresh piece of young grass with those tender shoots that are real food.

Litter for houses may be made up of equal parts of peat moss and sand or sifted earth, dried leaves, straw chop or bracken. Sawdust is sometimes recommended, but I would not use it, neither is dried grass a suitable material.

Why is sawdust not advised ? The answer is simple : On the score that we should waste nothing, it is only correct to assume that spent litter removed from a house will be used as a fertiliser for the kitchen or flower garden. Any gardening expert will agree that manure with a wood basis can easily spread fungus—and who wants this in his garden ? Apart from this drawback I know of no other reason why sawdust should not be used.

Making an Earth Floor

From the above it will be seen that floored houses are preferable to those without. An earth floor is very nice provided it is made correctly. This is how to do it : After removing the top spit of earth ram the rest as hard as possible and do not hesitate to use rubble to provide a solid base. The earth which has been removed should then be sieved back with a liberal mixing of coarse river-bed sand to help keep it broken down. With regular rakings, the removal of soiled parts and occasional replenishing with fresh siftings, such a floor will keep fresh for years.

Concrete floors are not advised, but droppings boards beneath the perches are essential no matter what type of floor is used. Such fixtures are a first-rate aid to the collection of manure, hygiene and the preservation of scratching litter. The days of a small trench beneath the perches to act as a manure pit are as dead as the dodo.

Keepers of large fowl might possibly wonder whether bantams could be mixed with the big ones ; they can, but it is a practice that few would advise. It is far better to adhere to the principle that each class of domestic poultry is best kept separately.

Here is one of the most popular types of bantam house—known familiarly as the six-by-four, it can be used either as an intensive or semi-intensive house. Main measurements are given in both photograph and sketch. Outside nest boxes, seen at ground level to the right of the photograph, allow approximately one square foot of floor space for each division. Sliding shutters (either solid or glassed) are fitted on the front. Internal fittings and measurements are in the sketch below.

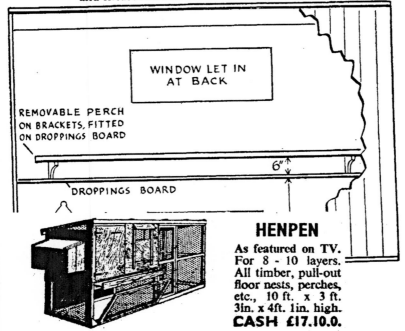

WINDOW LET IN AT BACK

REMOVABLE PERCH ON BRACKETS, FITTED ON DROPPINGS BOARD

DROPPINGS BOARD

6"

CHAPTER III

BREEDS AND THEIR VARIETIES

PRACTICALLY every large breed is duplicated in bantams. Rhode Island Reds, Light Sussex, Leghorns, Minorcas and Anconas, Wyandottes, Welsummers, Barnevelders, Plymouth Rocks and Hamburghs are only a few. Game fowls are represented by Old English, Indians and Moderns. Others that have yet to make their appearance are Marans, Campines and Orpingtons. It is interesting to note that the last mentioned is definitely " in the making " over here and has been established on the Continent for a number of years.

There are also breeds of bantams that are not seen in big fowl. The most outstanding example is probably the Sebright, a very beautiful little bantam which is found in two varieties—Gold and Silver ; the Japanese in a variety of colours, is another. A distinct feature of the Sebright is that the males are hen feathered and are thus devoid of saddle hackle and flowing tail.

Helping the Nation

The point has now been reached where a distinctive line has to be drawn. This book is a wartime publication ; its primary object, as previously indicated, is not the preservation of various breeds of bantams. It is written solely to direct attention to the purely utility varieties, varieties which, with correct management, will help in the task of food production.

No breeder of Modern or Old English Game, or of Japanese, Sebrights, Pekins or Rosecombs would claim that any of these enters the utility sphere. Even the producer of exhibition White Wyandottes would think twice before recommending his favourites. But Sussex, Rhode Island Reds, Anconas, Minorcas, Buff Plymouth Rocks, Columbian Wyandottes and a few others have every right to a place in our wartime programme.

It is a pity that the Sussex has gone no further than the Light and Speckleds ; Reds or Buffs would make notable additions. Speckleds have been in the making for a number of years, and definite strains have now been established. Barred Plymouth Rocks are also few and far between, while I do not remember seeing a White Rock.

Barnevelders and Welsummers are still in their infancy, and it is clear from those that have been seen that the Indian Game has been used in making the former while Old English figures in Welsummers. Strangest of all is

Egg in the centre is from a Rhode Island Red-Light Sussex large fowl cross. Admitted, it is a pullet egg, so also are those surrounding it, but they are from Light Sussex bantam pullets. Weight of large egg 1¾ ounces, the others average 1½ ozs.

the Leghorn family. We have a few White and Black Leghorn bantams, fewer still of Browns, but no Duck-wings, Cuckoos, Buffs, Exchequers, Piles or Blues. What an excellent opportunity there is here for makers of breeds !

These Breeds Lead

In the utility section, therefore, I would place Rhodes, Light Sussex, Anconas, Minorcas, Columbian Wyandottes, Buff and Barred Plymouth Rocks, with a corner for breeds like Buff and White Frizzles, Barnevelders, Welsummers and Black or White Leghorns.

The Game breeds, with Sebrights, Japanese, Hamburghs, Cochins, Rosecombs, White, Black and Buff-Laced Wyandottes, I would place in the " fancy " section. I shall probably be told that I have made mistakes—well, we all do that sort of thing at some time or another and I am always open to correction.

Beginners in bantams are not going to find their requirements in any of the breeds easily met. Limited numbers of matured birds are always available, but they are very limited indeed. Day-old bantam chicks are very seldom sold, while growing youngsters are almost unheard of. Eggs, however, are different, and in the breeding season many offers are made. My frank opinion is that the majority of beginners, for the time being at any rate, will either have to start with a breeding pair or a trio or with a

Here is one of *Poultry World's* utility appliances seen by many thousands of prospective poultry-keepers at the London Zoo. Originally designed as a brooder or cockerel box it can be used also as an intensive bantam house. If you like the layout and build your own allow as much floor space for each bird as possible. Removable tray at end is filled with peat-moss litter. Centre slide has a solid duplicate for use in cold weather.

sitting or two of eggs. Main thing is, of course, that a start is possible.

In pre-war days the bantam breeder left it late before putting his eggs down for hatching. June and July were, in fact, his favourite months. But he was not so much concerned with egg production. Newcomers desiring winter eggs are advised to allow approximately the same time for a bantam to mature as would be given to a large fowl. This means March and April hatching.

CHAPTER IV

FEEDING—WITH OR WITHOUT " BALANCER "

THIS chapter is an important one, so many questions having to be taken into consideration. It is, of course, just as illegal to feed bantams on foodstuffs fit for human consumption as it is to feed any other class of livestock, while the restrictions on " balancer meal " are such that one could not decide to commence in bantams today and draw rations for them tomorrow.

In case there should be any doubt on this point, let me again repeat that, in the eyes of the rationing authorities, a bantam is regarded as a domestic fowl and is entitled to precisely the same amount of rations as a large hen. This statement is, of course, made subject to strict observance of the regulations relating to the surrender of shell-egg registrations.

Therefore, to draw rations for six female bantams of over two months of age the domestic poultry keeper would have to surrender six shell-egg registrations to his local food controller. The advantage he gains is that the ration of balancer meal which he would receive would go farther among bantams than it would among large fowl.

Problem Partly Solved

I am not, however, so much concerned with " balancer meal." The more of that we can save the more food will be made available to the man who has to make his living out of poultry. I want to show that a few bantams can be maintained without any calls being made upon " balancer," and also without transgressing the law in so far as human foodstuffs are concerned. This is made possible only by the fact that bantams are such small eaters ; so small, indeed, that the most oft committed mistake is over-feeding.

A meal for six bantams reads very much like an extract from a cookery book—a cupful of this and a spoonful of that, and so on.

Only a few days before settling down to this little handbook I visited one of our best known South Country breeders of bantams. He was feeding his birds at the time of my arrival. On what?—Potatoes released for animal food. " There you are," he said, " the little devils prefer those to mash ! " Potatoes were not, of course, their only food, but in this instance they were playing an important part in the maintenance of a valuable stud.

What else can we call upon? Here is a list—Stale bread and crumbs unusable in the house, cake and pastry leavings, small pieces of meat or fish, left-over gravy and soups, scrapings of the breakfast, tea and dinner plates, soured milk or the remainders of milk puddings, bacon and cheese rinds. Beside these are the dozen and one things that the kitchen garden will provide : Chat potatoes, potato peelings, cabbage and lettuce leaves, a carrot or two, swedes, turnips and what not.

And don't let us overlook the food that the bantams find for themselves if they are given the outings in the garden or in their portable run on the lawn mentioned in a previous chapter.

A Satisfying Drink

The reader might well ask what use gravy, soup and soured milk would be if we have nothing in the way of cereal meals to dry them down with ? The answer is, give it to them to drink and reserve the crumbs for mixing in the soft food. The soup or gravy might need thinning down with warm water, but both are food and not a drop should be wasted.

How much food each day does a bantam need ? If it takes ten ounces of wartime mash to sustain a big fowl, a bantam will thrive on a third of that quantity. Three to four ounces a day of the pick of the above scraps, plus liberal helpings of minced or whole greenfood, will be more than enough for any bantam. Most households can save more than this and all that is necessary is to pick them over and blend the balance into appetising meals.

Where there happens to be a surplus never be tempted to give a little extra. Twenty minutes at the food trough is enough for a big hen and it is enough also for a bantam.

Twice each day is the order, morning and evening, with a mid-day " scratch " or helping of greenfood.

One thing with bantams is very necessary—mince all their food finely, and disregard the ridiculous advice that raw potato or raw potato peels are as good food as those that are cooked. Starch molecules, which are 90 per cent. of the food value of the potato, can only be broken down by cooking. The excuse that " my birds laid just as well on raw potatoes as they did on cooked ones " is very tame. They would probably have laid just as well without the potatoes at all, because it is certain that the raw potatoes passed through the birds in an undigested or partly undigested state. Give most other things raw, but not " spuds." No fuel need be wasted in cooking—bake them in the ashes beneath the fire-grate.

Fine mincing is necessary to avoid crop troubles ; it also helps considerably when the food passes into the gizzard. Bantams need grit in the same way that big fowl do—coarse sand or fine limestone for the chicks and a medium grit for the grown birds is best. A little limestone flour twice or three times a week in the soft food helps to provide the calcium for bone making and maintenance—a tea-spoonful for six birds is enough. This means that a pound of limestone flour will last for months.

Vitamin Deficiencies

Cod-liver oil will make up many vitamin deficiencies. Half a pint of oil used at the rate of a tea spoonful for every eight or nine birds twice a week will also last for months.

Let me now get down to a typical meal for six bantams : One mashed potato of medium size (or its equivalent in potato peelings), a tea-cup full of minced greens or swede, a couple of table-spoonfuls of meat or fish scraps (including minced gristle or soft fish bones, bacon or cheese rinds), an egg-cup filled with soured milk, soup or gravy, a handful of sifted " balancer meal " or waste bread or cake crumbs, a sprinkling of limestone flour, a few drops of cod-liver oil and we have more than enough !

This is a perfectly fresh meal and the leavings at breakfast time can go towards the evening meal without any risk of scouring through sourness. If that which is left should smell sour when the next feed is due, throw it away and mix a fresh lot.

Here is another meal : Leavings from the breakfast table (a few crusts of bread dried and powdered, the odd spoonful or two of porridge that baby refused to eat, rinds of bacon cut up finely), left-overs from lunch or dinner (these will be mainly cooked vegetables, possibly a few odd meat or fish scraps and, perhaps, the scrapings of a dish of rice pudding). Mix them all together and add two or three ounces of sifted " balancer " as a drying-off agent.

An occasional all-vegetable dish will be appreciated by the bantams. Here is a sample : A carrot or two finely minced, a cup-ful of grated swede, a few boiled chat potatoes with an odd leaf or two of lettuce or cabbage, or the minced tops of a few spring onions. Mix well together and feed in a trough.

There are, of course, one or two unrationed foods that the bantam keeper can purchase, outstanding among them being biscuit meal. This is a very excellent food, in spite of its somewhat high price. A small quantity, soaked overnight in milk bottle rinsings or left-over soup, makes almost a complete meal in itself. If a few meat scraps are available use them at the same time.

Turning Waste into Food

Correct method of preparing the waste crusts is as follows :—Break the crusts and small pieces to about the size of a sixpenny piece and put them all in an old baking tin or dish on top of the kitchen grate or on the plate rack of the cooking stove. When the pieces are thoroughly dry pass them through an ordinary household mincer. These small pieces powder down easily and they store and keep for weeks in a biscuit or other comparatively airtight tin.

Bantams simply love an odd scrap or two of meat. Watch them peck a bone clean—tie it firmly to the side of the run and it will keep them occupied for hours. Don't throw the bone away when it has been cleaned, put it in the salvage bag, or, if you are the fortunate possessor of a steam-pressure cooker, render some of the smaller bones to pulp and feed them in the soft food of the bantams.

One point about pressure cooking bones is worth observing. As soon as the bones have been softened, and following their removal from the cooker, they should be broken down while still warm. Allowed to get thoroughly cold they become ossified and are sometimes almost unbreakable again.

Small bones can sometimes be powdered down without the aid of a pressure cooker. Bake them in the oven at the same time that meals are being cooked and then pound them down with a hammer.

Substitutes for Grain

Another aid to occupation, apart from hanging cabbage leaves in house or run, is to impale a piece of swede on a blunted nail at the side of the run. The birds will remove every vestige of swede, leaving only the hard outer shell. Stems of kale similarly treated also make excellent food.

Grain we have none. But that does not mean we cannot find substitutes somewhere. Sunflower seeds and beech nuts are not ideal, but they can certainly be used. Crack them well and feed at the rate of three ounces for six

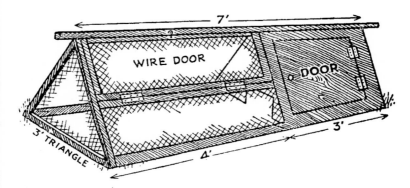

A Morant type of rabbit hutch lends itself well to the bantam-keeper. The normal wire-netted floor to the run is not necessary, while a double thickness of string netting can take the place of wire on the remainder of the appliance. Four to five bantams could be kept in an appliance with the above measurements.

bantams two or three times each week. Acorns can also be used in moderation. Gather a supply of these, store them in a dry place, and prepare for use as required. Here is the way to use acorns :

Remove the tough outer skin, break the inner halves of the acorn into small pieces, dry them in the residual heat of the oven or on the kitchen range and feed on alternate days to the sunflower and beech nuts. Do not overdo the acorns, two ounces for six birds is sufficient. When these substitute grain foods are given as a meal it may be necessary to supplement them by a limited helping of soft food.

The reader will observe that no mention whatever has been made of fruit. I have very strong ideas on this question, and they are backed by years of observation and the experiences of others. If windfall apples or pears were a penny a bushel I should not buy them to feed to birds in my care. The reason for this is that I have seen far too many cases of birds wasting away in orchards to run the same risk with my own. Very small helpings may be quite all right, but to show my dislike still further for this class of foodstuff I shall not attempt to define what these helpings should be.

Feed Mashes Crumbly

From the foregoing it is plain that our bantams are far from being dependent upon official rations and that good wholesome food can be found for them without transgressing the law. All that is required is a fair measure of commonsense in the preparation and mixing of these foods in a manner that makes them palatable.

Outstanding facts to bear in mind are : Feed the mashes crumbly rather than sloppy ; cook all potatoes or potato peels ; waste not a drop of soup or gravy ; solicit the help of neighbours so far as bread scraps and crumbs are concerned ; remember that apart from insects found in the garden, the only animal food that bantams receive will be the meat and fish scraps, and animal food is most essential for their welfare ; never be tempted to use fruit waste and try always to keep the birds busily occupied.

CHAPTER V

BREEDING AND CHICK REARING

NOT everyone will want to breed their own bantams, but, knowing hobbyists as I do, I am certain that even some of our wartime beginners will want to try their skill as stock producers. And it is here again that bantams differ from large fowl—they do not want wide, open spaces and lots of grass range to breed successfully, but they do appreciate a *small* grass run. Not only do they appreciate it, but the natural food that such a run provides is an excellent aid to fertility.

Correct season for bantam breeding is from May to the end of Summer. This is chosen by breeders so as to keep size down by compelling the young stock to rear in the coolness of autumn and the cold of winter. If, for utility purposes, the wartime breeder desires to commence his season earlier, there is nothing to stop him ; an April start will find his pullets in lay long before the following Christmas. Bantams, incidentally, take about the same time to mature as large fowl ; a good general average age for starting to lay is eight months.

Two and a Male

A breeding pen can be made up of almost any small number of birds—a cock to two pullets or a cockerel to six or seven hens. Try, whenever possible, to have age on one side of the pen. The experienced breeder will use cockerels with pullets, but he practises some of the tricks of the trade which may be beyond the technical knowledge of the beginner. Remember also that the established breeder may still be working on a reduction of size, a point which will not unduly concern the wartime utilitarian.

Mate the birds about a month before eggs are required for sitting and do not hesitate to take the little male on one side for a special feed on his own now and again. He may be courteous and refuse it because his hens are not with him, but if he takes kindly to this " extra " it will prove an excellent aid to fertility ; best thing for him are tiny scraps of raw meat.

Before proceeding further I want to warn beginners not to expect every egg to be fertile or every fertile egg to give a strong liveable chick. In the first place, the foods we are using are not of the right type for breeding ; there is always a tendency towards over-fatness and this is not, by any means, helpful in chick production. Secondly, we must appreciate the fact that bantam chicks are tiny compared with ordinary chicks and are thus not so strong.

Another point to bear in mind is that, while the eggs can be artificially hatched, the chicks cannot be artificially reared nearly so successfully as when under a hen. It may be wise, therefore, to adhere to natural methods throughout. A little bantam hen will cover eight of her own eggs and will mother her chicks with infinite care ; a big fowl will take up to 18 or even 20 eggs and mother every chick that hatches from them. When a large fowl is used chose a medium sized bird of not too clumsy a type.

Shorter Incubation Period

Period of incubation is less than that with large fowl— 19 days to be precise, although it is always wise to allow the full 21 days if the hatch does not commence earlier.

To get back to the breeding stock. Respect the request made earlier in this handbook, keep the breeds pure and leave crossing and sex-linkage to the commercial side of the industry. Bantams are not a commercial possibility and crossing can easily defeat the object for which they were produced.

General rules of incubation should be closely followed. Use only the freshest of eggs, let the hen sit in a not too dry but well sheltered and secluded corner, test out on the eighth or ninth day and discard infertiles, broken yolks or addled eggs.

Losses among chicks must be expected, while, without the orthodox foods to rear them, the percentage loss is certain to be higher than would normally be expected. For this reason it is doubly necessary not to tolerate any weaklings ; these weaklings are certain to pick up any trouble that comes near to them and they are an ever-present danger to the remainder of the flock.

Refrain from feeding the chicks for the first 24 hours after hatching. Then start them off on the tastiest morsels that our scrap foods can be made to provide. Reserve one or two eggs from the adult stock for feeding and do not hesitate to use infertiles as food for the youngsters. Do not, however, make the mistake that most people make when feeding eggs, that is, giving them to the birds in a

Elaborate coops and runs are not needed for bantam chicks. Main thing with them is ease and portability. Overhead protection in case of rain is provided either by boards or a canvas sheet. Ordinary fish net of double thickness can easily replace the more orthodox wire netting.

hard-boiled state. Hard-boiled egg taxes the digestive powers of the chicks beyond endurance and the correct way to feed this food is to use either the egg raw or very lightly boiled.

Very Little and Often

If the rule with big chicks is to feed little and often, then that for bantams must be *very* little and often. An egg-cupful of food properly prepared is enough for a dozen chicks at each meal when four feeds are given daily.

If it is possible to obtain some of the cod-liver oil biscuit food normally used for cage birds, get it and use it for the bantams. A couple of spoonfuls of this or, alternatively, some of our waste crumbs in which a spot or two of cod-liver oil has been mixed, will dry off half an egg and provide a very sustaining meal.

Very finely minced greenfood can be introduced early to the chicks and one of the best of these that I know is the tops of young spring onions. Dandelion leaves are also valuable food. It will possibly read ridiculous when I write that the tops of two or three onions or a similar number of dandelion leaves are ample for a dozen very young bantam chicks ; this quantity should, of course, be increased as time progresses.

There is no need to become worried if the youngsters are seen helping themselves to the food given to the broody hen, but for safety's sake make certain that her meals are finely minced. For grit use coarse river-bed sand at the start and a very fine grade limestone after the chicks are a week old. A pinch or two of limestone flour at each meal is a necessity.

Give Chicks Preference

For once in a while, deprive the older birds of any milk that happens to go sour, and of that odd spoonful or two of rice or milk pudding that baby refused to eat. Let the young bantams have all that can be spared of either of these foods and leave out coarser house-scraps until their use is almost forced upon you. A spoonful of very finely minced dog or cat meat helps a lot, so also will a little rich meat gravy.

Nothing in the preparation of a dainty meal should be too much trouble for the bantam chicks, but keep the amounts given to them ridiculously low so as not to tire them of their food.

One thing above all else—keep the bantam chicks away from coarse tough grass. Nothing I could mention can cause crop troubles quicker than those odd pieces of dried grass which, strangely enough, appear to hold a particular attraction for young chicks.

CHAPTER VI

MISCELLANEOUS HINTS—COMMON AILMENTS

PERCHES for bantams are best when made out of 1½-inch squaring. Allow a minimum of six inches space for each bird and round off the upper corners of the perch so that, when it is in position, a section of it resembles an inverted " U."

A spare set of perches is an asset. While one lot is in use the others are cleaned up and their ends soaked in creosote. This is probably the best method of keeping

Runs of the type shown here play an important role in bantam keeping. Especially is this true where grass is available. The house shown would, in normal times, accommodate a stock cockerel, but it is also ideal for a bantam hen and chicks or a trio of layers.

them free of red mite. Make the change-over every week or every other week.

Nest boxes need be only nine or ten inches square. Place them in a secluded corner of the house and allow one box for every four birds ; straw chop or peat moss is probably the best nesting material. The danger with hay is that some of it may be eaten and lead to crop troubles.

Shallow feeding troughs, barred across the top to

prevent the birds from scratching out the food, should allow five or six inches feeding space for each bird. A double-sided trough two feet in length will accommodate eight birds.

Bantams simply love to take their food straight from a grass run and, in suitable weather, the mash can be pressed together into lumps about as big as a walnut and spread over an area of clean grass. No matter how finely it is eventually broken down, the bantams will clear up every bit of it.

An outstanding feature with any breed of bantam is tameness. Once they become accustomed to their owner they become extraordinarily tame and, while they like to wander, a low fence usually keeps them within bounds. Ordinary string netting of about three to four feet high is quite strong enough to keep bantams under control. Should any of them show a desire to explore a neighbouring garden all that is necessary is to " ring " their run with a strand of very thin wire fixed in position about six inches above the upper strands of the netting. A bantam only needs to fly into this strand of wire once.

Treat Only Minor Ailments

I do not propose to fill pages of this book with descriptions of ailments and their cure. Any illness, excepting those of a minor character, should not be tolerated among bantams. It is for this reason that an earlier chapter says weaklings should not be persevered with.

A common cold, or a slight case of leg-weakness in a matured pullet, will quickly respond to treatment. Anything more serious, such as a cold which turns to roup, or leg-weakness which is rickets and not leg-weakness at all, should find the owner prepared to kill.

Bantams are not immune to those diseases which attack large fowl, but, given special management and well-ventilated quarters, they possess extraordinary powers of resistance when taking their smallness into account.

To avoid colds go to any length to make the roosting quarters comfortable, but do not do as some do—convert the roost into an almost air-tight box. Fresh air is essential and, so long as it does not reach the birds in the form of direct draughts, it must be provided for. Ingress for this air will be provided by the pop-hole entrance and by controllable slots immediately beneath the droppings board.

These slots, cut in the house, will be lined on the inside by a strip of perforated zinc similar to that used for small meat containers. On the outside wooded groves will accommodate glass slides which are regulated according to the amount of air necessary. Instead of slots a series of 1-in. holes can be similarly protected and controlled.

An excellent idea is seen in the " Seaford " house. Half-a-dozen 1-in. holes, an inch apart, are cut in the side of the house and to break the entrance of fresh air a sheet of tin is bridged over them.

Foul air exit must be at the highest part of the house. In a lean-to a small space where the front of the house meets the roof, and for the entire length, will serve admirably. In an apex type the air exit would, of course, be at the ridge.

Common in Warm Weather

To get back to common colds. These, strangely enough, are not as prevalent in mid-winter as they are in mid- or late summer. Immediately a sneeze is heard the victim should be removed from the pen, isolated and treated. Bathe its nostrils in warm water lightly coloured with a few permanganate of potash crystals. Squeeze out of the nostrils any gathered mucous and then, with a small brush of the type used by children for water paints, dress the nostrils with oil of eucalyptus. Repeat this treatment morning and evening for three or four days to effect a complete cure.

Leg-weakness referred to may only be a light attack of cramp. Remove the cause—excessive dampness in house or run—dress the legs with sweet oil and give the victim an extra drop or two of cod-liver oil.

Crop troubles have frequently been mentioned in preceeding chapters. If, despite the adoption of precautionary measures that have been outlined, they do make their appearance, treat them in this way : Give the affected bird half a tea-spoonful of medicinal paraffin, then, gently but thoroughly, break up the impaction in the crop.

During treatment withhold all solid food, giving the bird nothing but a little milk to drink ; if the milk is sour so much the better. Within a day or so the trouble should disappear.

Intestinal worms seem to regard bantams as favourite hosts and an occasional drive against them may be made. Feed a very light meal early in the day and another as the final meal in the afternoon. In this second mash mix thoroughly a half-tea-spoonful of powdered areca nut for every six bantams. First task early the following morning will be to clean the droppings board and so remove any worms that have been driven out. If worms are seen repeat the treatment ten days later ; if none are there the bantams are probably not affected.

Another minor trouble common in bantams is scaly leg. Wash the lower part of the legs, the only part which is affected, in hot soapy water and then dress them either with sulphur ointment or vaseline in which a few drops of paraffin have been mixed. Be particularly careful not to allow any of the paraffined vaseline to spread to the fleshy part of the leg.

Watch for Insects

Give the bantams an occasional light dusting with insect powder as a safeguard against body lice. Parts deserving special attention are beneath the wings and the fluff around the abdomen.

One other statement needs confirmation. In the introductory chapter I referred to table properties of the bantam. These properties are, of course, limited to *petit poussins*, and I can assure readers that surplus cockerels can be made into most appetising meals.

Segregate the little fellows at an early age, pen them on their own, give them as much of the coarser types of food that are left after picking out the best for the layers and kill for table purposes when they turn the scale at 16 ounces. It will be found that they skin much easier than pluck.

A wartime dish introduced by bantam breeders is bantam pie—a glorified edition of pigeon pie, and glorify is the best description that can be given to it. I know, because I have had some ! Unfortunately I am not a cook, but most housewives have a pigeon pie recipe.

Yet a further delicious dish is fried chicken. A plump little bantam cockerel, plus a rasher or two of bacon and some piping hot chipped potatoes, should satisfy the most fastidious eater.

If an older bantam cock or hen is to go to table, a little hint worth following is to add a few drops of vinegar to its food each day for two or three days prior to killing. This helps to transform a boiler into a roaster.

But this chapter must not be a copy of " Mrs. Beeton." I am certain that the average housewife needs no prompting from me to invent dainty dishes in which surplus bantam cockerels can play a major part.

Egg Preservation

To conclude this chapter, let us look once again to the egg returns. Bantam eggs preserve just as well as ordinary hen eggs. They can be put down either in waterglass or by the use of any of the proprietary dry systems of preservation. Should matters reach the stage when neither of these are obtainable use the following method :

Mix well together equal weights of lard and boracic powder. Lightly grease the palms of both hands with some of this mixture and roll each egg to be preserved between the palms sufficiently thorough to place a thin film of the mixture over the whole of the shell. Wrap each egg in a small piece of greaseproof paper (margarine wrapping is excellent) and store in a cool place until needed for use. Eggs treated in this manner keep well for months.

If waterglass is used the liquid should not be disturbed once it has thickened off. Where " dry " systems are employed the eggs must be stored in a cool corner and an occasional turning is advantageous.

I have endeavoured in this handbook to help beginners in bantams through their initial problems. It is not, by any means, a standard work on miniature fowl ; such a work must come from a pen more capable than mine.

I am convinced that bantams can be made to play an important part in essential food production. Even if they do nothing more than provide eggs in return for food that would otherwise be wasted I think the end will justify the means.

But they will do more than that. They will provide their owner with many hours of interesting relaxation of a type that is far removed from other hobbies ; he is given the opportunity to create something that is not mechanical, but something that will continue to hold his interest when food shortages remain only a grim memory.

Domestic Fowl Proper

At the risk of being told to revise my ideas, I would definitely class the bantam as the domestic fowl proper, leaving large varieties in the hands of small-holders and professional farmers. They fit well into a small garden scheme and, after the full effects of the war have worn off, when we can relax a little from our present aims—eggs— there will be no reason why our utility pens should not give way to something more ornamental in nature.

It is then, I hope, that we shall see more of those beautiful little Sebrights, tall and graceful Modern Game, broad-breasted but perky Indians and many of the other breeds and varieties whose names do not even appear in this small book.

Let me issue a warning : Once the show " fever " attacks the bantam hobbyist he will never be able to ward it off. For all time he will be despatching his birds here, there and everywhere and anxiously waiting their return with the much coveted red or blue " ticket."